TANGLED ROOTS

Tangled Roots

Samantha Orchard

Sunlit Speaks

This book is dedicated to family, in all its forms.
Our roots might be tangled, but they make us who we are.
Thank you for keeping me grounded.

we were girls together

purple pixies forever:
feral, wild, grinning and free
barefoot, fearless, yelling through the woods
chasing fireflies and catching frogs
faces lit up by the glow of a bonfire
falling asleep in the grass

weekends full of magic and laughter:
fairy portals, secrets on a playscape
stories whispered in the dark
while our parents laughed over drinks
innocence untouchable
before the world taught us not to be soft
our own secret club

oh, to run through the woods with you again
fingers linked in pinky promises
eyes lit with wonder
daydreaming with our heads together
gazing up at the clouds

Youth

all scraped knees
dirt smudged face and sun-kissed skin
hanging upside down from trees
bare feet running over gravel roads
through puddles and grass

exploring the marshes like a second home
a feral child-queen with a crown
made from leaves and sticks
tossing stones in the canals

half savage, all wild,
armed with wooden swords
when each day felt like a lifetime
when a dirt road and a back yard
felt like the whole world

Family Ties

shady dirt road running to the river
lined with willow and maple trees
marshes stretching toward the horizon
phragmites and cattails turned gold
five children in a three bedroom house
dreaming of tomorrow

walked along the ice as a child
each step a thrill of danger and joy
created fairy tales in the back yard
watching everyone I loved get older
until I did, too

tempered the teachings of my parents
with my sister's compassion
my eldest brother's wanderlust
my middle brother's caution
and I'm reckless like my Irish twin
I wonder what they learned from me

CSCSD

courthouse walls closing in
I'd never felt so small
in my best dress that I never wore again
shaking like a leaf

made my mom cry as I told it again
fifteen gets you twenty
but nine only got you fifteen
had to relive it for strangers
while you looked at me with murder in your eyes

but in the end did it even matter
when you'll be a free man next July
and I still wake up screaming
feeling your hands around my throat?

Comment Section

Nathan says:
oh you're only fifteen?
but so mature for your age
and you look so much older
you'll get me in trouble
just look so much like a woman

James says:
you look great in that dress
you'd look better on your knees

Jacob says:
do you even know the band
on that poster in the background?
I hate girls like you, fucking posers
bet you can't even name two of their songs

Mark says:
hey girl you're pretty cute
you single? you up? dtf?
hey. hey. answer me.
I said answer me bitch!

[this photo has been removed.]

unlove letters: vol 1

the first sparks of a bonfire
counted the miles between us
tried to fold them like paper planes
and fly home

a daydream through telephone lines
faded into oblivion
lost in the fever
of troubled teenage minds

lyrics and letters
led to silent resentment
for a pedestal I felt trapped on

TOO YOUNG

called me angel with his hand at my throat
trembling and afraid in the dark
he tore the pages from my favorite books
introduced my head to the bedpost
left marks where nobody would see them
and I'll never understand it

the smell of sweat and tobacco
the sound of his voice ringing in my ears
every time I close my eyes
has me shaking in fear even now
haunts my heavy head
brings me back to nine years old
struggling to get away

things I can't forget meet
the things I can't remember
blanks in my memory leave me angry
because a man wanted something
he had no right to take

a three year long nightmare
left me with questions
that'll never be answered

16//Bright

snapshot: ferris wheel
teenagers laughing in the language
of the forever young and invincible
sulfur, smoke, and cotton candy
vivid colors exploding through the dusk

snapshot: back road
all the windows down in a pickup
homemade mix cd in the stereo
bouncing over potholes and gravel
five kids in a four door

snapshot: garage show
music so loud our teeth hurt
screaming over the bass and drums
mosh pit bruises we wouldn't feel
until the next morning

to be sixteen and fearless
dressed in arrogance and hope
was a gift and a burden
all at once

Not a Suicide Note

checking out and breaking down
darkness breaks across haunted eyes
as my strength wears down

you're long gone, my hope unfulfilled
tell me dear what is left of you?
who will i name these butterflies for
to keep my hand from grasping a blade?

and if i give in to the roaring in my veins
let that crimson whisper release
would you spare me a second glance
or finish the job for me,
twisting the knife you left in my back?

hurricane

he told me that he was a natural disaster
and i told him i could handle it.

i guess i forgot that a single girl
can't withstand the force of a hurricane,
that when the levees break so does your heart

i guess i forgot
the way anger can rise like a tidal wave
and hit like a lightning storm,
and how when your entire being goes up in flames
all the bridges you're standing on burn too

unlove letters: vol 2

lightning from the blue
whispers from something like heaven
the closest thing to God
you said you'd ever seen

stealing kisses in the hallway
hands in your pockets
left me aching for destruction
begging to be struck down
where I stood

cut off my hair and your family
but kept the shirt

Final Feedback

is it brutal or honest to admit
that you are my one regret
despite how the softness of your kiss
still lingers on my cheek
like sunlight through a dirty window

and even now that i feel nothing
the taste of your betrayal coats my tongue
like old coffee long since burnt
you were in lust, but i was in love
and i was too naive to know the difference

never again

Growing Pains

out here alone, snow covers everything
the nights are silent and cold
looking up at the merciless sky
blue black, studded with a million stars

one more year
and this small town will be a memory
I'll be off to college
away from everything I've ever known
thought thrills and terrifies me:
don't know how to live without
the sky sweeping wide and open
above quiet streets and starlit backyards

but I have to go in order to grow
the world is bigger than this map dot
and I've been itching to explore it
all my life

Sapphic

I wanted to drink you in like water
breathe you in like air
your touch burning in the best way
you and the lines of fire down my hips
world exploding in a burst of sweetness
from the taste of your kiss

soft skin, velvet lips, roving hands
slip them under your sweatshirt
grab my waist, pull me in
bring me closer to heaven
touch you with reverence
a goddess in worn out blue jeans

fall to my knees at your feet
tangle your fingers in my hair
let me worship at your altar

Beginnings

weightless
floating through space untethered
dappled twilight through the leaves
cotton candy clouds
painted in pink and purple
shot through with the soft orange glow
of the setting sun

watch the moon rise gracefully
dusk spread out like a blanket
break the walls down
been a long time coming
but we're looking at the same sky

spend the afternoon lost in conversation
fold up the mile markers like paper planes
use them to fly home to you

Late Night//Early Morning

12:03 am
we exchange words, verbal ballet
keeps you dancing through my thoughts
long after the conversation ends

12:18 am
"It's what friends do."
you smile over Skype
but we aren't just friends,
soon we'll be lovers
hands searing skin, lips locked
lost in the moment

12:24 am
heart racing, make a mess of me
can't breathe for the thought of you

12:37 am
I'm trying so hard not to overreact
but you're the sun
and I'm the moon;
I reflect the light you give me
and I just can't look away

Tropes

be the brightness in the break
daydreaming in intimacy and smoke
lover's caress to a friend's embrace
follow the line and watch it curve
into dangerous territory

let the dream linger
into waking hours
won't you please wreck my plans?
feel your eyes on me when I look away
light another candle, pull another card
still more questions than answers

slipping down under the gravity
of the thoughts you inspire
I've got a dirty mind, babe
and lately you've been on it

Lines//Blurred

my hand finding yours
backlit by the computer screen
your laughter fills the air
and your fingers lace through mine
smile on your face
thumb running over the back of my hand

my head finding your shoulder
our eyes met
mine closed
your lips on mine and
our hands all trembling
hearts racing long past midnight
sweet fire of whiskey
lingering on our tongues, in our throats

my hands in your hair
and your fingertips
tracing down my spine
warmth of your hands on my bare back
made me shiver
your touch melting away
the ice in my veins

unlove letters: vol 3

sharp thorns like a rose:
open up, watch me unravel
singing to soothe the panic attacks
swore to keep the demons away

half drunk in your mother's living room
dancing until we collapsed
laughing on the floor

you said the world is cruel,
so's everyone in it
but somehow, somehow not me
too intense to hold
we drained each other dry

Grown Ups

we moved here nearly a week ago;
we got a run down duplex
in a sketchy part of town

we carried boxes
up a flight and a half of stairs
I brushed the hair off my cheeks
threw open the curtains
let the sounds of the city filter through
I never see the stars anymore,
but its fine

this college town and these city lights
remind me of the things I want to be:
not a girl who could never be enough
not fanciful or foolish
but determined to make the city mine

Roommates

high in the living room
on the hand-me-down couch
all the windows thrown open
desperate to catch a breeze
the intense heat of late August
seeping into our bones

we were laughing
as you put french braids in my hair
getting me ready for my first college party
packing bowl after bowl
Phantom of the Opera on the TV
guitar filtering through the windows
from a lesson downstairs

talking about music and work
classes and exams
when all we had to worry about
was making it through the semester

Rulebook

keep your keys between your knuckles
pepper spray in your purse
when you leave the house remember-
you're prettier when you smile

don't go out alone after dark
get a roommate and a dog
check every backseat
you climb into
keep the police on speed dial

lose the extra five pounds
don't forget to do your makeup
leave the hair on your head long
you're prettier that way
but make sure the rest of your body
is soft and smooth as silk

dress well but keep in mind
if your skirt's too short you're asking for it
there's safety in numbers
but not in a crowd

exist as a woman
and watch yourself burn out

Blank Slate//Adulting

let me fall like these autumn leaves
spiraling around you in the sunlight,
brilliant colors against the sky

a strange beauty haunts these streets
I fall in love with the sounds of the city
when I walk home alone

everything is so much different-
from the traffic humming along the street
to the laughter spilling out from bars,
to the drugs and romance of midnight college towns

walk my city, let my cup of coffee warm my hands
Let It Be playing through my headphones
I wasn't born here, but I think I belong here

Winking Owl

we're getting wine drunk
on a Wednesday night
and everything is gonna be okay

pink moscato in gold rimmed teacups
sweet and tart, tastes like freedom
we're laughing, passing around the bottle watching Futurama,
talking about the intricacies of human nature

and our dryer doesn't work
and the kitchen outlet shorted out again
but everything's alright.
we're alright.

Cliff's Edge

barely breathing in beauty and bruises
with a sad smile on the face of a girl defeated
barefoot and alone by the sea

standing on the edge, eyes closed, she whispers to the wind
"oh my darling, my love, fly away home,
I know now your place is not by my side
fly away home, sweet blue-eyed betrayal,
but please, my love, remember me."

her smile fades as she drops to her knees
"forgive me for this, dear heart.
you were my forever. my dream.
am I still your only? your princess, your sweetheart?
your comfort, your love, your life?
or am I forgotten
just like the flower petals
left on my bed?
please, my love, forgive me."

she draws a deep breath, her eyes close
as she turns around,
and slowly lets herself
fall.

Beginning of the End

I never asked for this;
half empty beds
waking up to your absence
and the blankets all tossed aside

the wind shakes the windows
in their frames
you kissed my hair before you left
meant as both a good morning
and a goodbye

the room is hushed
our bed grows cold
and I get bitter
without you next to me

Burnt Bulb

you rise before the sun
you rub the sleep from your eyes
stumble to the kitchen
half drunk from the night before

brew a pot of coffee
listen to the silence of 5 am
and wonder how you got here
the world feels dim
nothing you do feels right

take another hit
face the fact that your life is in shambles
but you can't bring yourself to care.

you're just like every other 20 year old girl
losing herself in the city
dye your hair to set yourself apart
fall in love with romanticism and traffic

make it stop?

how much of me is made up of this?
desperation to make this stop hurting, searching for light in the darkness
waking in silence
to feel the weight of existence

years go by and shadows learn to speak:
reminders of a girl who no longer exists
did I once know her?
I can't believe I used to be her

girl turned ghost becomes nothing after all
and I'm screaming retaliation:
bright red lipstick rebellion
against the darkness

stood alone for so long
shouting till my throat was raw
"I will be loved, I will be wanted,
I am. I am. I am"

but then again...
maybe he was right

19//Loverboy

picked me up at midnight, half drunk
glow of your headlights lit the street
desperate kisses in the dark,
fourteen years too far to fall

white powder on your bedside table,
dressed up for you to undress
stale beer and cigarettes scenting your sheets
let that dress slide off my shoulders
pinned me down in the TV glare
blame it on the whiskey, on the molly

when you slapped me across the face
I begged you to do it again;
tasted blood and called it love

slipped from your bed at sunrise
walked across the city alone
washed the taste of you from my mouth

selfsabotage

am I the monster or the martyr
to sink my teeth into everything
I've ever loved

leave bits of my soul behind,
scattered like ashes
across the freshly cleaned floors
of every room I've ever walked through

think I'm broken somewhere down deep,
and I'm sure it can't be fixed
always causing chaos, destruction in my wake
clawing at the walls
of this cage I put myself in
slamming my fists against the door

I hand out pieces of myself:
give and give until nothing is left
what happens when this vessel runs dry?

The Road

been running from my past
found myself in the same places
lost and found all at once
I repeat the same dizzying cycles
drag my dead weight forward

brace my hands against the vanity
find my own eyes in the mirror
whispering to myself over and over
"this is just a moment
let it pass like all the rest"

now I'm standing on a bridge
soaked in gasoline
bending down to strike a match
not the first time I've watched
as my world went up in flames

hell, not even my first time causing it

unlove letters: vol 4

the meaning of passion
an addiction I couldn't seem
to wrap my head around
a long way to fall,
but your eyes like the ocean drew me in

short lived and furtive
whispering in the rain
laid in your bed to taste
the cigarettes on your lips
in the glow of a muted TV

let you worry yourself
right into my bones

Grapevine

I heard you were looking for me
in a stranger's bed
found nothing but the smell of my skin
soft and fleeting

You were a toxic wasteland
I found myself trapped in
begging in the night
"please no more"

You told me nobody would ever love me like you
and maybe that's true
but maybe that's the way I want it

Bluster//Gale

oh honey,
the earth is whispering to you
listen as the storm breaks

take a breath and gaze at the world around you
a forest draped in red and gold
the scent of snow kissing the air

early morning frost sugaring the ground
grey november steals october's glories
as it is, as it was, as it must be

Two of Seven

the city holds my secrets-
I walked those streets alone at night
wandering and wondering
and dreaming of home

college town, bright lights
the lost girl and her fairy tales
waiting for someone to save her,
she swears tomorrow will be the day

but I slipped out of a stranger's bed
and woke up older
got four lines of molly lined up neat,
and the train tracks are beckoning

lost girl ran home again,
tail between her legs
between lust and pride,
can't tell which did her in

Too Close

can't breathe
nobody's fault but my own
whole body shaking like a leaf
fight, flight, freeze or fawn:
if I can't choose one
I'll attempt them all

and I'll end up on the floor again
clutching my head in my hands
sobbing wildly in the silence
of an empty house
I can't take a compliment
but I can damn sure take a beating

the girl in the photos is dead
and I killed her
sacrificed her on an altar of twisted bone
to the god of broken things
an act of devotion
for the straws that broke my back

Trauma Bond

our hands are bloody
gripping roses so tightly in clenched fists
that the thorns are embedded
in the flesh of our palms, weeping blood
down each stem

keep shrinking me down to size
cross the lines till they crumble
brittle bones tinged with crimson
silent pleas for ruination
no less than we deserve

heads bowed, hands clasped,
sending prayers to a god
who never listened in the first place

Philosopher's Stone

the swelling ache
of these brittle bones breaking
my cup has run dry and yet I remain:
ashamed to take, therefore I give

and ride the tides of emotion
let them break against the shore of my body
I've never been a saint
but I'd bleed myself out to be a martyr
let my wings melt, doomed by pride
to come crashing back down
for the sin of daring to reach for the sun

hush your complaints, girl:
you've never been an alchemist
who are you to think
you could turn lead to gold

goodnight

fell asleep with socks on
just to wake up with cold feet
like the way you must have
the day you left

was desperate to fix you
shouldn't have tried

you left your scent in these sheets
your name engraved in my bones
baby, I fell asleep waist deep in love
and woke up lost and empty

Grand Rapids

staying in a motel on Alpine
everything I own in bags
packed away in the car

slept on your friend's living room floor
three weeks in a row
we fought and overstayed our welcome
you wanted to call the cops
and they kicked us out

spend hours in the library
just trying to keep warm
gloves are threadbare
bitter wind cuts through my coat

walk to the bus stop
watch my breath crystallize
and I want to go home
but I don't know where that is anymore

Kiss Me, Kill Me

will you miss me coming home to you
under neon lights smiling
and my breath caught up in my throat determined to break my heart

or maybe you'll miss the sparkle in my eye
or the laugh I offer when there are no words
and maybe your smile will keep me awake,
but then again darling,
maybe it won't.

what if one morning you let your eyes open
sunshine playing havoc against your wall
as you slowly come to realize
I am not there
no sleeping girl beside you

tell me all you know and all you are
open old wounds,
show me all your bruises
as I walk away
a bullet in the chamber
your heart in my hands

Don't Come Back

my hair is a different color now
from when you tangled your hands in it
and I'm laughing freely,
although it makes my ribs ache

it's taking time, but I'm learning to be better
now I'm worlds apart
from the shell that I was-
came home with her heart broke
and head hung low

they say the cells of the body
replace themselves every seven years.
If that's so, in seven years
I'll have a body that has never been beneath yours.
and isn't that a blessing.

rabid dog

"where does it hurt?"
everywhere

bare my teeth in an empty threat
roll over with a whimper
showing my belly instead of some spine
cower in the corner
shaking at the thought of being free

let the fear send me trembling
tail between my legs
clinging to the past
watching gold go up in flames

run right back to the hands
that drain me dry
brittle bones aching for something
I don't know the name of
leave me foaming at the mouth
convulsing on the floor

Bound for Home

go home for a time
in cold October air
where my brother lights my cigarettes
as we chat about the weather

he's dropping hints
that I should come home for good
while I pull my gloves from my pocket

but I've seen mountains
shared movie nights under southern stars
laughed and cried and learned my way
through the last nine months

how do I dare come "home"
when it feels like I've always been on the road?

Core Memory

Hand in hand at the roller rink
sweet sixteen, first double date
you convinced them to play Pierce the Veil
over the speakers
Bulletproof Love and we sang every word

Loser by Beck is blasting on the highway
you're pounding on the dashboard
of your older brother's Bonneville
trying to keep the radio working
our friends laughing in the back

prom night in that pretty purple dress
I still have the pictures somewhere
me looking at you like you hung the moon
you looking over my shoulder at her
danced with your brother and your friends
while you disappeared in the crowd

I haven't thought about you in years now
but I still have that red flannel
from our first date
reminds me of sweet sixteen,
being in love for the first time

Mourning Dove

hands held out
to catch the fireflies
flickering out in the darkness

waves are crashing on a distant shoreline
and somewhere,
there are lovers on a rooftop
whispering intimacies in the rain

there is faith and there is hope
there are things we do not see
oh, my little bird,
trust your wings, not the branch.

A Letter to Addiction

are you listening? or
am I just radio static on a station
too far out of range
winter feels endless and
hope's feathers have fallen

slipping through your fingers
sand in an hourglass
rain on the window
the silence is deafening and
the candles all went out

where do we go when we go
please just tell me he wasn't alone

Order Up

the popular kids grew up too-
they're laughing at the bar
while I'm wiping down counters:
I see them through the kitchen pass
throwing back shots

I've been home three years
and I'll never get used to it
makes me remember locker room taunts
and bus stop snickers

they don't recognize me,
and I don't know if that's a blessing
or a curse

21320

white walls, the smell of disinfectant
wheelchair rolling down a noisy hall
feel the IV slip into my arm
saline dripping cold into my vein
can't stand the pain or the dizziness
so I'll fade out of the twilight,
let the darkness take over

I'll stay here forever,
but I don't know that right now:
in and out, voices a blur
desperate and afraid and weak

this moment stretches eternal,
plays out the same way every time:
blood loss and bruising
a five thousand dollar hospital bill
jagged pieces of my heart
that'll never fit back into place

vices

finding myself at the bottom of a bottle
was never part of the plan
but here I am staring down at this whiskey
pretending it doesn't burn going down
acting like I'm fine

head in hands, take another hit
glass clinks against the table
cigarette smolders to ashes
been holding on till may for twelve years
and I've made it to another
pushing through the mess and the stress
looking for myself in a haze of smoke

I'm bitter I never got the chance
to be a normal kid
angry at the necklace of bruises
given by a man who knew better
and scars I'm afraid
I'll never be able to stop opening

Happy Mother's Day

what a strange misery it is
to mourn something that barely existed
in the first place
coping with humor only works
until you run out of jokes

there and then gone
with nothing to show
except blood running tacky down your legs
nails bitten down to the quick
a hospital bill you can't afford
a life that never was

2AM//Dark

lord knows I wasn't blessed with patience
and god damn, I'm burning this candle at both ends
so where's the fucking light?

thinking back to sixteen and reckless
nineteen and careless
twenty one and lost.
to the could-have-been's and
the never-will-be's
and the no-more-chances.
when the last door slammed in my face,
I just couldn't find a window.

so I light the candle again.
just a little more, honey.
watch those flames burn out right along with me,
but at least you'll be warm.

Introspection

I. you learn how to disappear into the woodwork at 16. how to slip through life unnoticed, but not unbothered. how to mind your p's and q's, write in a journal instead of with crimson and silver against pale skin.

II. you learn how to dance on bars at 19. wild and reckless and off on your own. vision blurring, thin white lines in a bathroom stall. the streetlight casting a glow across his face when he slapped yours and you begged him to do it again.

III. you learn to hold your own hair back at 22. when the world is spinning and it's all you can do to hold tight to that porcelain. when it's long past midnight and you just don't know how to face the morning.

IV. but morning comes whether or not you're prepared for it. so go to sleep. things look different in the daylight.

Honesty

sometimes it's me
that's the problem

can't pretend I haven't been toxic
I've broken my share of hearts
trying to fix the people around me
when it was me who needed fixing
early twenties in a bitter haze
blaming everybody but myself
for all my problems

stings to admit it
but I wasn't always a good friend
selfish and jealous, petty and stubborn
giving away different versions of myself
like candy on Halloween
going ghost for the smallest slight
borderline unhinged

can't change the past
or un-burn the bridges
that I set aflame
just wake up in the morning
and try to be better than I was
the day before

Holloweyed

made up of shaky hands,
we haunt these dirt roads
blowing silver from dandelions
watching grass sway with the breeze

everyone's looking for somewhere to run

same old stomping grounds,
church parking lots and alleyways
where teenagers furtively hide their cigarettes
behind cupped palms,
smoke rising like prayers turned skyward

so few stop lights in this town
but we've blown through all of them:
laughing wildly in the back of a pickup
or sobbing in a passenger seat
got older, just never grew up.

PTSD

get over it get over it get over it
oh gods it's been so long since I've felt like this- pull the trigger

FLASHBACK: in the bathroom -
the smell of woodsmoke and
that awful wintergreen tobacco and
my brothers arguing from the other room
over whose turn it was to pick the movie;
completely unaware that he's got
his hands around my throat

FLASHBACK : in the woods -
crying and begging with no voice
running with legs that won't move
carried me back to camp
"she fell asleep at the fire
she's so silly, I'll put her to bed"

FLASHBACK: in the living room -
"There's no way. I refuse to believe my son
would do anything of the sort
and if he did you must've asked for it
must've wanted it"

Willow, Evergreen

if part of me is still standing here
in the dust kicked up by truck tires
watching the storm roll in over the river
to paint the world in shades of blue
will it ever leave?

the years may have passed in a blur
but each day feels like a lifetime
walk the streets I grew up on
seeing ghosts around each curve

remember how we dreamed of getting out
but I came back, I came back
to the tangled roots of home

this place is the same as it ever was
but I'm forever changed

Cross Streets

21 and gratiot
your hand on my knee
singing along to jack & diane
on the radio

just freeze time right there baby
summer sun and the windows down
falling in love from the passenger seat
who knew we were one right swipe away
from the rest of our lives

keep me in this moment
sunlight through cigarette smoke
kiss me at every red light
think I'll marry you someday

la petite mort

new day dawning
beyond the rush of august nights
wrap your fingers around mine
through the give and the take
of a tender morning

and he hits his knees
worships like the faithful
at the altar,
like my body is a holy place
he can't get enough of

trace lines of fire down my skin
liquid velvet fills the room with light
breathes me into his lungs
sweetness before the shatter

tied down

you put a star on my finger
said you pulled it from the sky
brushed the hair out of my face
whispered sweetness in my ear

darling I had a dream that we were dancing
slow and easy under ballroom lights
kiss my cheek and hold me closer
count me in for forever

I'll let you tie those cords
tight around our wrists
pick the colors and the flowers
I'll meet you at the altar in white

Woman's Work

button shirts at the collar
to keep them from distorting
hang them in a neat row in the closet
it'll keep away the wrinkles
sweep the floors and write the shopping list
never enough hours in the day
to get the to-do list done

and I'm finding myself in my mother's shoes
locked in by the lessons
handed down generation after generation
expectations of what a woman should be
where she should go

and I remember her shaking her head
when I was six years old
saying like her mother before:
"you can't trust a man
to do woman's work"

HAUNTED

dissociative and dizzy and freezing
like a ghost in my own home
I haunt the silence
my brain's a mouth full of teeth
eating through the wires of memory
leaving them mangled and tangled
till I can't differentiate between traumas
till one image bleeds into the next
a constant kaleidoscope of horror and hurt

and even fifteen years later
I still wake up crying in a sweat
recoiling from the thought of being touched
I still scrub myself raw
in an effort to feel clean
my body was a temple
and they fucking desecrated it

Arcana II

I watched the foundation crumble,
now the tower is crashing down again
king lost his crown, i tore out the page
now I'm looking for stars
in a clouded sky

the hermit in her cave
sorting cards one by one
accepting the things she can't change

with a sword in each hand
I'll play the fool
push through the dark
until I can touch the sun

Riverbed

can we walk down to the water
need the wind in my hair
and the sun on my face
need laughter ringing through my ears
and the pier below my feet

want to watch the ice melt with spring thaw
want to feel fresh and new and clean
as the swans come back to the marshes
and the freighters make their way down the river
bound for places I'll never go

let our cigarette smoke hang in the crisp air
inhale doubt and exhale peace

Rural

we all swore we'd get out of this town
now we're scuffing our shoes
in the same old parking lots
bumming cigarettes and talking trash
treading water, trying to stay afloat

the fishermen crowd the bay
they all say it'll be a dry summer
cursing the smell of smoke in the air
from the countryside burning a river away;
it's a small world, and we're all trapped in it

party store clerk watched us grow up
trading fruit snacks and ice cream
for rolling papers and liquor
shoot the breeze, same old same old
he doesn't bother asking for our IDs

we're settling like dust
in the town we grew up in

peach moscato

took it too far again
head spinning, seeing double
holding to the porcelain like a lifeline
a glass became a bottle
became my cheek against the cool tile
of a bathroom floor

from giggling to crying in seconds
hating every part of myself
but I do this every time
spin the screw top off
say goodbye to a quiet night

no excuse, can't explain myself
never mean to get that drunk
but here I am again
staring up at a popcorn ceiling
trying not to be sick
bathroom floor growing warm beneath me

Inner Child

I am constantly grieving
the little girl in the photograph
on my parent's dresser
with warm brown eyes wide in awe
staring at the lizard in her arms
like it's the most amazing thing in the world

scraped knees and missing-tooth smile
back before the hurt
when the world was one dirt road wide

she's still here somewhere
I'm going to find her again.
and I will keep her safe.

is this growth?

but i can still feel your hands around my throat, dear.
won't you come a little closer,
look at me in the light?
really see what i've become.

they say time heals everything,
but i lay awake and think about the light you snuffed out
my hands still shake when i light my cigarettes

i am better without you.
i am free.
yet i can't stop looking over my shoulder.

Rearview Mirror

pour me out like wine
gather the pieces of my heart
thrown like flowers at a wedding
down countless aisles and avenues
wherever they ended up,
could you please send them back

don't think I'll ever learn to let go
not in the right way
I'll run back to the people who hurt me
until my tear ducts are dry
look for the good in them
even when I know there's not enough

call it a savior complex
hell, call it codependency
but given the choice
between you and a grudge…
I'll hold you every time

Circle//Sisterhood

hold out your hands
as we drift through life
keep me anchored
though we might never meet

show me what it is
to be a good friend
despite juggling children, jobs, marriages
let me learn from you
what it means to be a woman
regardless of who you are
or what path you walk

silver and gold, circles unbroken
not sisters by blood
but choice

quarter life crisis

let these years slip through my fingers
a decade just water under the bridge
dancing with the ghosts
of everyone I've ever been
and everyone I thought I'd become

but it's late august again
and I'm pacing the kitchen
wearing holes in the linoleum floor
too busy fretting over what I haven't done
to see just what I've accomplished
lighting my candles at both ends

the bridges give way beneath the weight
of me and my twenty five unfinished selves
add another year to the pyre
I'm older
but am I better?

Solace

bare trees like skeletons against the sky
leaves scattered across every sidewalk
frost on the grass in the mornings
a world growing colder

I come alive with the autumn
November wind through my hair
dancing in the glow of the streetlights
let the grey skies make me whole

turn my face to the clouds
and wash the guilt from my bones
for a life lived on my own terms

Marshlands

muddy water in my veins
lungs filled with choking phragmites
planted wildflowers in my soul
to grow out along the cage of my ribs
trace delicate patterns of roots
like ivy through the brick of my being

sing to me in blazing star and prairie grass
let the green fade into gold
chorus of birds and frogs melds together
soothes my trembling hands
clog the waterway with lilies
bring peace with the breeze
paint hope with the dawning sun

scent of nectar hangs in the air
air sticky-sweet and heavy
walk the paths of my childhood
until the girl I was is standing beside me
until the woman I'll be is before me

ACKNOWLEDGEMENTS

This book would not have been possible without the love and support of the people I hold dear. I am both honored and privileged to be surrounded by some of the most wonderful individuals I've ever had the pleasure of meeting, and I wish I had the space to name you all. Nobody is truly self-sufficient- after all, no man is an island, and without my community, I wouldn't be where I am today.

I'd like to sincerely thank my good friends Emery Austin and Chaiya Sirgany for their time and skill in editing. Several of the pieces in this collection were inspired by prompts written by the incredibly talented Lex Lynn, who you can find on Instagram as @poems.bylex.

I'd also like to thank the communities I'm a part of; from family to the lovely people I've met online, particularly the Denettes and the r/weed discord server. All of you are truly incredible, and I am so beyond blessed to know you.

Finally, I'd like to thank *you*, the reader, for giving this book a chance and letting me share this piece of my heart with you.

Milton Keynes UK
Ingram Content Group UK Ltd.
UKHW020748141123
432548UK00016B/923